The Wiersbe

BIBLE STUDY SERIES

The
Wiersbe
BIBLE STUDY SERIES

COLOSSIANS

Become the

Whole Person

God Intends

You to Be

David C Cook®
transforming lives together

THE WIERSBE BIBLE STUDY SERIES: COLOSSIANS
Published by David C Cook
4050 Lee Vance View
Colorado Springs, CO 80918 U.S.A.

David C Cook Distribution Canada
55 Woodslee Avenue, Paris, Ontario, Canada N3L 3E5

David C Cook U.K., Kingsway Communications
Eastbourne, East Sussex BN23 6NT, England

The graphic circle C logo is a registered trademark of David C Cook.

All Scripture quotations in this study, unless otherwise noted, are taken from the
Holy Bible, New International Version®. *NIV*®. Copyright © 1973, 1978, 1984 by
International Bible Society. Used by permission of Zondervan. All rights reserved.

In the *Be Complete* excerpts, all Scripture quotations, unless otherwise noted,
are taken from the King James Version of the Bible. (Public Domain.)

All excerpts taken from *Be Complete,* second edition, published by
David C Cook in 2008 © 1981 Warren W. Wiersbe, ISBN 978-1-4347-6780-6

ISBN 978-0-7814-4567-2
eISBN 978-0-7814-0628-4

The Team: Steve Parolini, Karen Lee-Thorp,
Amy Kiechlin, Jack Campbell, and Susan Vannaman

Series Cover Design: John Hamilton Design
Cover Photo: iStockphoto

Printed in the United States of America

First Edition 2009

6 7 8 9 10

121814

Contents

Introduction to Colossians

The Church

Colossae probably would never have been mentioned in the New Testament had it not been for the church there. The city is never named in the book of Acts because Paul did not start the Colossian church, nor did he ever visit it. Paul had heard of their faith (Col. 1:4, 9), but he had never seen these believers personally (2:1). Here was a church of unknown people, in a small town, receiving an inspired letter from the great apostle Paul!

The Colossian assembly was predominantly Gentile in its membership. The sins that Paul named (Col. 3:5–9) were commonly associated with the Gentiles, and his statement about the mystery applied more to the Gentiles than to the Jews (1:25–29). The church was probably about five years old when Paul wrote this letter.

The Heresy

What was the heresy that threatened the peace and purity of the Colossian church? It was a combination of Eastern philosophy and Jewish legalism, with elements of what Bible scholars call gnosticism. This term comes from the Greek word *gnosis,* which means "knowledge."

To begin with, this heresy promised people such a close union with God that they would achieve a "spiritual perfection." Spiritual fullness could be theirs only if they entered into the teachings and ceremonies prescribed. They also believed in a state called "full knowledge," a spiritual depth that only the initiated could enjoy. This "wisdom" would release them from earthly things and put them in touch with heavenly things.

It is easy to see how this kind of teaching undermined the very foundations of the Christian faith. These heretics attacked the person and work of Jesus Christ. To them, He was merely one of God's many "emanations" and not the very Son of God come in the flesh.

The Letter

In his letter to Colossae, Paul used the vocabulary of the false teachers, but he did not use their definitions. He used these words in their true Christian meaning. As we study Colossians, we will find words such as *fullness, perfect, complete,* all of which were used by the gnostic heretics.

His main theme was the preeminence of Jesus Christ (Col. 1:18; 3:11). There is no need for us to worry about angelic mediators or spiritual emanations. God has sent His Son to die for us! Every person who believes in Jesus Christ is saved and is part of His body, the church, of which He is the head (1:18). We are united in Christ in a wonderful living relationship.

Once he had established the preeminence of Christ, then Paul attacked the heretics on their own ground. Wrong doctrine always leads to wrong living. Right doctrine should lead to right living. In the two concluding chapters, Paul applied the preeminence of Christ to the daily affairs of life.

The Bottom Line

Many Bible scholars have concluded that Colossians is the most profound letter Paul ever wrote. The church today desperately needs the message of

Colossians. We live in a day when religious toleration is interpreted to mean "one religion is just as good as another." Some people try to take the best from various religious systems and manufacture their own private religion. To many people, Jesus Christ is only one of several great religious teachers, with no more authority than they.

This is an age of syncretism. People are trying to harmonize and unite many different schools of thought and come up with a superior religion. They are not denying Christ, but they are dethroning Him. As we study this exciting letter, we must heed Paul's warnings: "Lest any man should beguile you" (2:4 KJV); "Lest any man spoil you" (2:8 KJV); "Let no man therefore judge you" (2:16 KJV).

—Warren W. Wiersbe

How to Use This Study

This study is designed for both individual and small-group use. We've divided it into eight lessons—each references one or more chapters in Warren W. Wiersbe's commentary *Be Complete* (second edition, David C. Cook, 2008). While reading *Be Complete* is not a prerequisite for going through this study, the additional insights and background Wiersbe offers can greatly enhance your study experience.

The **Getting Started** questions at the beginning of each lesson offer you an opportunity to record your first thoughts and reactions to the study text. This is an important step in the study process, because those "first impressions" often include clues about what your heart is longing to discover.

The bulk of the study is found in the **Going Deeper** questions. These dive into the Bible text and, along with excerpts from Wiersbe's commentary, help you examine not only the original context and meaning of the verses but also modern application.

Looking Inward narrows the focus down to your personal story. These intimate questions can be uncomfortable at times, but don't shy away from honesty here. This is where you are asked to stand before the mirror of God's Word and look closely at what you see. It's the place to take a good look at yourself in light of the lesson and search for ways in which you can grow in faith.

Going Forward is the place where you can commit to paper those things you want or need to do in order to better live out the discoveries you made in the Looking Inward section. Don't skip or skim through this. Take the time to really consider what practical steps you might take to move closer to Christ. Then share your thoughts with a trusted friend who can act as an encourager and accountability partner.

Finally, there is a brief **Seeking Help** section to close the lesson. This is a reminder for you to invite God into your spiritual-growth process. If you choose to write out a prayer in this section, come back to it as you work through the lesson and continue to seek the Holy Spirit's guidance as you discover God's will for your life.

Tips for Small Groups

A small group is a dynamic thing. One week it might seem like a group of close-knit friends. The next it might seem more like a group of uncomfortable strangers. A small-group leader's role is to read these subtle changes and adjust the tone of the discussion accordingly.

Small groups need to be safe places for people to talk openly. Through shared wrestling with difficult life issues, some of the greatest personal growth takes off. But in order for the group to feel safe, participants need to know it's okay *not* to share sometimes. Always invite honest disclosure, but never force someone to speak if he or she isn't comfortable doing so. (A savvy leader will follow up later with a group member who isn't comfortable sharing in a group setting to see if a one-on-one discussion is more appropriate.)

Have volunteers take turns reading excerpts from Scripture or from the commentary. The more each person is involved even in the mundane tasks, the more he or she will feel comfortable opening up in more meaningful ways.

The leader should watch the clock and keep the discussion moving. Sometimes there may be more **Going Deeper** questions than your group can cover in your available time. If you've had a fruitful discussion, it's okay to move on without finishing everything. And if you think the group is getting bogged down on a question or taken off on a tangent, you can simply say, "Let's go on to question 5." Be sure to save at least ten or fifteen minutes for the **Going Forward** questions.

Finally, soak your group meetings in prayer—before you begin, during as needed, and always at the end of your time together.

Miracles and Prayers

(COLOSSIANS 1:1–12)

Before you begin …
- *Pray for the Holy Spirit to reveal truth and wisdom as you go through this lesson.*
- *Read Colossians 1:1–12. This lesson references chapters 2 and 3 in* Be Complete. *It will be helpful for you to have your Bible and a copy of the commentary available as you work through this lesson.*

Getting Started

From the Commentary

The apostle Paul was a great encourager, and this epistle is a good example of the grace of thanksgiving. In this section (which is one long sentence in the original Greek), he gave thanks for what Christ had done in the lives of the Colossian Christians.…

Like Paul, we should be grateful for what God is doing in
the lives of others.

—*Be Complete,* page 29

1. What does Colossians 1:3–12 teach us about encouragement and prayer?
How does Paul go about encouraging the Colossian Christians? How might
these words have been received by those who were dealing with the gnostic
heresies described in this study's introduction (pp. 7–8)?

*More to Consider: The gospel was brought to Colossae by Epaphras, a
citizen of that city. Epaphras probably came in contact with Paul during Paul's three-year ministry in Ephesus. What does the way in which
Epaphras responded to Paul's message say about how we, as Christians,
ought to share our testimonies with others?*

2. Choose one verse or phrase from Colossians 1:1–12 that stands out to you.
This could be something you're intrigued by, something that makes you uncomfortable, something that puzzles you, something that resonates with you, or just
something you want to examine further. Write that here. What strikes you about
this verse?

Going Deeper

From the Commentary

> The theme of this epistle is the preeminence of Jesus
> Christ, and He is certainly preeminent in the gospel. The
> false teachers who had invaded the fellowship in Colossae
> were trying to remove Jesus Christ from His place of pre-
> eminence; but to do this was to destroy the gospel.
>
> —*Be Complete*, page 30

3. In 1:3–12, what assumptions does Paul make about the Colossian Christians and their understanding of the basics of the gospel? How does Paul
introduce the theme of Christ's preeminence in 1:3–12?

From the Commentary

> Paul said that the gospel was bearing fruit in all the world.
> The Word of God is the only seed that can be planted
> anywhere in the world and bear fruit. The gospel can be
> preached "to every creature which is under heaven" (Col.
> 1:23). Paul's emphasis was on "every man" (Col. 1:28).

False teachers do not take their message to all the world. They go where the gospel has already gone and try to lead believers astray. *They have no good news for lost sinners!*

—*Be Complete*, page 32

4. In Colossians 1:6, Paul states that the gospel is bearing fruit all over the world. Why do you think Paul emphasizes this to the church at Colossae? How does a larger perspective on the impact of the gospel help Christians who are struggling with controversial doctrines, as the Colossians were?

From Today's World

Although we live in a global society, with access to world events merely a mouse click or a channel flick away, many people today have a sort of "tunnel vision" when it comes to issues within their workaday world. This could be anything from a limited perspective on the issues facing the business they're in to a myopia regarding broader concerns in their churches, communities, or even their families.

5. What leads a group of people (or even individuals) to miss the bigger picture in life? Why is a broader perspective (a global view, for example) helpful in understanding local concerns? What are some of the key issues

Christians face today that demand a broader view in order to gain a realistic perspective? In what ways was Paul encouraging this same sort of view in Colossians?

More to Consider: The teachers who had come to Colossae came with the intent to undermine the saints' faith in Christ. What are some examples of this sort of false teaching going on today? What are some of the best ways to determine if a teacher is presenting a "false gospel"?

From the Commentary

Epaphras did not simply lead the Colossians to Christ and then abandon them. He taught them the Word and sought to establish their faith. The word translated "learned" in Colossians 1:7 is related to the word *disciple* in the Greek language. It is the same word Jesus used: "Learn of me" (Matt. 11:29) or, in effect, "Become My disciple."

—*Be Complete*, page 34

6. Colossians 1:7–8 speaks of Epaphras's role in the Colossian church. What can we suppose about his role based on what Paul writes? What does this say about Paul's relationship with Epaphras? About how the gospel is spread?

More to Consider: The word disciple *is used more than 260 times in the Gospels and Acts, and the verb translated "to learn as a disciple" is found 25 times in the New Testament. As you go through Colossians, circle all the references to discipleship (learning, etc.). Why do you think Paul emphasizes this theme? What are the implications of this idea for today's church?*

From the Commentary

Love is another evidence of true salvation, for the unsaved person is wrapped up mainly in himself (Eph. 2:1–3). The fact that these people loved *all* the saints was proof that God had changed them and given them eternal life. Christian love is not a shallow feeling that we manufacture; it is the work of the Holy Spirit in our hearts (Rom. 5:5; Col. 1:8). It is worth noting that Colossians 1:8 is the only

verse in the letter that mentions the Holy Spirit, and it is
in connection with love.

—*Be Complete*, page 36

7. Paul mentions the Holy Spirit only once in Colossians (1:8). By contrast, he speaks of Christ repeatedly. Possibly the false teachers in Colossae were playing up the Spirit or spirit(s) at the expense of Christ. Why might emphasizing the Spirit/spirit and de-emphasizing Christ be attractive to some people? What's could go wrong when emphasizing the Spirit and de-emphasizing Christ?

From the Commentary

The false teachers promised the Colossian believers that they would be "in the know" if they accepted the new doctrines. Words like *knowledge*, *wisdom*, and *spiritual understanding* were a part of their religious vocabulary, so Paul used these words in his prayer.

—*Be Complete*, page 43

8. What does Paul say about knowledge and wisdom in 1:9–10? Why is it significant that Paul repeatedly uses words like *knowledge* and *wisdom* in this letter? How is the false teachers' promise of greater knowledge similar to the temptation Satan offered in the garden of Eden?

More to Consider: Wiersbe writes that "thankfulness is the opposite of selfishness." How does Paul speak to this theme? What are some examples from real life that prove this to be true?

From the Commentary

It is God's energy that empowers us. Colossians 1:11 reads, in effect, "With all power being empowered according to the might of His glory." Paul used two different Greek words for God's energy: *dunamis* (from which we get our word *dynamite*) means "inherent power"; and *kratos* means "manifested power," power that is put forth in action. The grace of our Christian lives is but a result of God's power at work in our lives. Spiritual growth and maturity can come only as we yield to God's power and permit Him to work in us.

—*Be Complete*, page 49

9. What does it mean to be "strengthened with all power" (v. 11)? What is the significance of the explanation that follows, "according to his glorious might"? What, according to Paul, is the purpose of this strengthening? How is this like what Christians today are called to be and do?

From the Commentary

> The Colossian epistle is filled with thanksgiving. Paul gave thanks for the church in Colossae (Col. 1:3), and he prayed that they might grow in their own thanksgiving to God (Col. 1:12). The Christian life should abound with thanksgiving (Col. 2:7). One of the evidences of spiritual growth in our Bible study is thanksgiving (Col. 3:15–17). Our prayers should always include thanksgiving (Col. 4:2). The Christian who is filled with the Spirit, filled with the Word, and watching in prayer will prove it by his attitude of appreciation and thanksgiving to God.
>
> —*Be Complete*, page 52

10. Go through this first section (1:1–12) and underline or list every "thankful" comment Paul makes. Given that Paul's readers were facing

difficult times, why do you think he went out of his way to thank them and thank God for them? How might the Colossians have responded had Paul started right off with challenges to the questionable doctrines? What role does true thankfulness play today in encouraging others toward a right doctrine?

Looking Inward

Take a moment to reflect on all that you've explored thus far in this study of Colossians 1:1–12. Review your notes and answers and think about how each of these things matters in your life today.

> *Tips for Small Groups: To get the most out of this section, form pairs or trios and have group members take turns answering these questions. Be honest and as open as you can in this discussion, but most of all, be encouraging and supportive of others. Be sensitive to those who are going through particularly difficult times and don't press people to speak if they're uncomfortable doing so.*

11. Paul uses a lot of this section to encourage the Colossian Christians. In what ways do Paul's words encourage you? How would you feel if you received a letter like this when you were struggling with theological or

personal faith issues? What does this say about how we, as Christians, ought to reach out to others who are facing challenges?

12. Paul makes special mention of Epaphras in the introduction, thanking him for all he's done to build up the church. Who are the teachers and leaders who have made a positive impact in your faith life? How have you shown them your appreciation? Why is it important to acknowledge those who help us grow in faith? How does doing this glorify God?

13. What are some of the ways you've been tempted to embrace questionable doctrines? Why is the promise of "a greater knowledge" so tempting to Christians? How do you go about testing the scriptural validity of claims made by supposed Christian leaders? If you've fallen for false doctrines in the past, what led you down that path? How did you find your way back to the truth?

owow segment.

Going Forward

14. Think of one or two things you have learned that you'd like to focus on in the coming week. Remember that this is all about quality, not quantity. It's better to address one specific area of life and do it well than to work on many and do poorly (or to be so overwhelmed that you simply don't try).

Do you need to learn how to be more encouraging? Do you need to explore more about the basics of faith so you won't be tempted to follow false doctrine? Be specific. Go back through Colossians 1:1–12 and put a star next to the phrase or verse that is most encouraging to you. Consider memorizing this verse.

Real-Life Application Ideas: Go to those people who have been your greatest teachers and encouragers in the faith, and offer them some encouragement of your own. Write a thank-you note or send them a gift to say "thanks" for all they've done in your life. If you're a member of a small group, consider doing this for your group leader, too.

Seeking Help

15. Write a prayer below (or simply pray one in silence), inviting God to work on your mind and heart in those areas you've previously noted. Be honest about your desires and fears.

Notes for Small Groups:

- *Look for ways to put into practice the things you wrote in the Going Forward section in this lesson. Talk with other group members about your ideas and commit to being accountable to one another.*
- *During the coming week, ask the Holy Spirit to continue to reveal truth to you from what you've read and studied.*
- *Before you start the next lesson, read Colossians 1:13–20. For more in-depth lesson preparation, read chapter 4, "Crown Him Lord of All!" in* Be Complete.

Christ's Preeminence

(COLOSSIANS 1:13–20)

Before you begin …
- *Pray for the Holy Spirit to reveal truth and wisdom as you go through this lesson.*
- *Read Colossians 1:13–20. This lesson references chapter 4 in* Be Complete. *It will be helpful for you to have your Bible and a copy of the commentary available as you work through this lesson.*

Getting Started

From the Commentary

The false teachers in Colossae, like the false teachers of our own day, would not *deny* the importance of Jesus Christ. They would simply *dethrone* Him, giving Him prominence but not preeminence. In their philosophy, Jesus Christ was but one of many "emanations" that proceeded from God and through which men could reach God. It was this claim that Paul refuted in this section.

29

Probably no paragraph in the New Testament contains more concentrated doctrine about Jesus Christ than this one.

—*Be Complete,* page 57

1. After reading this section of Colossians, go back and circle the phrases describing Jesus. Why does Paul place this doctrine of Christ at the front of his letter? What are the key concepts Paul puts forth? How would each of these speak to a congregation struggling with false doctrines?

2. Choose one verse or phrase from Colossians 1:13–20 that stands out to you. This could be something you're intrigued by, something that makes you uncomfortable, something that puzzles you, something that resonates with you, or just something you want to examine further. Write that here. What strikes you about this verse?

Going Deeper

From the Commentary

> Man's greatest problem is sin—a problem that can never
> be solved by a philosopher or a religious teacher. Sinners
> need a Savior. [Col. 1:13–14] presents a vivid picture of
> the four saving actions of Christ on our behalf: He deliv-
> ered us; He translated us; He redeemed us; and He has
> forgiven us.
>
> —*Be Complete*, pages 57–59

3. What is the "dominion of darkness" Paul references in 1:13?

Paul describes succinctly why we need a Savior. Why is it important to
be reminded of Christ's supremacy?

*More to Consider: Read Matthew 18:21–35. How does this parable
support Paul's teaching on forgiveness? Why is the forgiveness theme
important to Paul's letter? How might the Christians who had been following the gnostic teachers have felt when reading about forgiveness?*

From the Commentary

> The term "firstborn" does not refer to time, but to place
> or status. Jesus Christ was not the first being created, since
> He Himself is the Creator of all things. "Firstborn" simply
> means "of first importance, of first rank."
> —*Be Complete*, page 60

4. In Psalm 89:27, God said He was appointing King David as His firstborn. In what sense was David God's firstborn? In what sense is Jesus the
Father's firstborn?

Read Hebrews 1:3 and John 14:9. How do these passages explain what
it means to call Christ "the image of the invisible God" (Col. 1:15)?

From the History Books

All sorts of sects in history have used Christian beliefs as a basis for their
theologies. One such group, the Christadelphians, which was started by Dr.
John Thomas (a British Congregationalist minister), claims to follow Christian doctrines but denies such things as the Trinity, Jesus' existence prior
to His incarnation, salvation by grace through faith alone, and the person-
hood and deity of the Holy Spirit. They also believe that Jesus had a sinful

nature. The Christadelphians are sincere about their faith, but their skewed perspective on some very basic biblical doctrines places them in a similar group with those who were leading the Colossian church astray.

5. Why is Jesus' sinlessness important to our Christian faith? Does sincerity in belief matter if the doctrines are wrong? Please explain your view. Why can we, as Christians, state without equivocation that belief systems like Christadelphianism are non-Christian?

From the Commentary

> Since Christ created all things, He Himself is uncreated. The word *for* that introduces [verse 16] could be translated "because." Jesus Christ is the Firstborn of all *because* He created all things. It is no wonder that the winds and waves obeyed Him, and diseases and death fled from Him, for He is Master over all.
>
> —*Be Complete*, page 60

6. One of the challenges the Colossian church was facing had to do with the gnostic teaching that Jesus was a created being. How does Paul refute this

in verses 15–16? What would be the effect on our Christian understanding of salvation if Jesus were a created being instead of God?

From the Commentary

"In him all things hold together" (NIV). A guide took a group of people through an atomic laboratory and explained how all matter was composed of rapidly moving electric particles. The tourists studied models of molecules and were amazed to learn that matter is made up primarily of space. During the question period, one visitor asked, "If this is the way matter works, what holds it all together?" For that, the guide had no answer.

But the Christian has an answer: Jesus Christ!

—*Be Complete*, page 61

7. As you read Colossians 1:13–20, what key words or phrases stand out to describe how Jesus is the glue that holds our faith together?

From the Commentary

> No denomination or local assembly can claim to be "the
> body of Christ," for that body is composed of *all* true believ-
> ers. When a person trusts Christ, he is immediately baptized
> by the Holy Spirit into this body (1 Cor. 12:12–13). The
> baptism of the Spirit is not a postconversion experience—
> for it occurs the instant a person believes in Jesus Christ.
>
> —*Be Complete*, page 62

8. Why might it have been of particular significance to the Colossian Christians that Christ is the head of "the body, the church" (v. 18)? Why is it
important to us today that Christ is the head of "the body, the church" and
not just the Savior of lots of individuals?

*More to Consider: Review Colossians 1:18. Why did Paul use the
word "born" in connection with death? How does this contrast help
explain what it means that Jesus was "first"?*

From the Commentary

> Paul had already called Jesus Christ "his [God's] dear Son"
> (Col. 1:13). Those who have trusted Jesus Christ as their
> Savior are "accepted in the beloved" (Eph. 1:6). For this
> reason, God can call *us* His beloved (Col. 3:12).
>
> Then Paul took a giant step forward in his argument,
> for he declared that "all fullness" dwelt in Jesus Christ!
> The word translated "fullness" is the Greek word *pleroma*
> (pronounced "play-ro-ma"). It was a technical term in the
> vocabulary of the gnostic false teachers. It meant "the sum
> total of all the divine power and attributes."
>
> —*Be Complete*, page 64

9. Paul states that God was pleased to "have all his fullness dwell in [Jesus]."
Why is the fact that God was pleased important to Paul's argument? What
sort of picture does this paint of God? Of His love for His people?

From the Commentary

First, Jesus Christ has taken care of *all things*. All things were created by Him and for Him. He existed before all things, and today He holds all things together. He has reconciled all things through the cross. No wonder Paul declared that "in all things he might have the preeminence" (Col. 1:18).

Second, all we need is Jesus Christ. We have all of God's fullness in Him, and we are "filled full" (complete) in Him (Col. 2:10). There is no need to add anything to the person or work of Jesus Christ. To add anything is to take away from His glory. To give Him prominence instead of preeminence is to dethrone Him.

Third, God is pleased when His Son, Jesus Christ, is honored and given preeminence. There are people who tell us they are Christians, but they ignore or deny Jesus Christ. "We worship the Father," they tell us, "and that is all that is necessary."

—*Be Complete*, pages 67–68

10. How does Paul's teaching about Christ in this section of Colossians lay a foundation for battling false doctrine? Go back through Colossians 1:13–20, and see if you can identify the specific places where Paul accomplishes what Wiersbe describes in the previous excerpt. In what ways can this passage of Scripture be helpful when we are talking with seekers?

Looking Inward

Take a moment to reflect on all that you've explored thus far in this study of Colossians 1:13–20. Review your notes and answers and think about how each of these things matters in your life today.

> *Tips for Small Groups: To get the most out of this section, form pairs or trios and have group members take turns answering these questions. Be honest and as open as you can in this discussion, but most of all, be encouraging and supportive of others. Be sensitive to those who are going through particularly difficult times and don't press people to speak if they're uncomfortable doing so.*

11. Have you ever been tempted to solve your problems apart from Christ? If so, what did that look like? In what ways does Paul's argument about the role of Jesus as Savior speak to those areas of your life you're tempted to solve through other methods?

12. As you think about your faith story, what doctrines have been the most difficult for you to wrap your head around? Why is it appealing in our culture to treat Christ as important but not in a class by Himself?

13. If you were approached by a group calling themselves Christians but who espoused questionable doctrines, how would you respond? What are ways you can test their doctrine for truth? How well can you explain your own beliefs? Why is it important to know what you believe?

Going Forward

14. Think of one or two things you have learned that you'd like to focus on in the coming week. Remember that this is all about quality, not quantity. It's better to address one specific area of life and do it well than to work on many and do poorly (or to be so overwhelmed that you simply don't try).

Do you need to become more familiar with the basic doctrines of Christianity? Do you want to better understand the pseudo-Christian cults that are in existence today? Do you need to spend time thinking about the ways Christ is supreme so that He becomes more than an accessory in your life? Be specific. Go back through Colossians 1:13–20 and put a star next to the phrase or verse that is most encouraging to you. Consider memorizing this verse.

> *Real-Life Application Ideas: Create a personal doctrinal statement, outlining your beliefs about key theological issues such as sin, salvation, and the person of Jesus Christ. You might want to work on this in a small-group setting or in a one-on-one meeting with a pastor or small-group leader. Support all of your statements with relevant Scripture.*

Seeking Help

15. Write a prayer below (or simply pray one in silence), inviting God to work on your mind and heart in those areas you've previously noted. Be honest about your desires and fears.

Notes for Small Groups:

- *Look for ways to put into practice the things you wrote in the Going Forward section in this lesson. Talk with other group members about your ideas and commit to being accountable to one another.*

- *During the coming week, ask the Holy Spirit to continue to reveal truth to you from what you've read and studied.*

- *Before you start the next lesson, read Colossians 1:21—2:3. For more in-depth lesson preparation, read chapter 5, "One Man's Ministry," in* Be Complete.

⊞Paul's Ministries
(COLOSSIANS 1:21—2:3)

Before you begin ...
- *Pray for the Holy Spirit to reveal truth and wisdom as you go through this lesson.*
- *Read Colossians 1:21—2:3. This lesson references chapter 5 in* Be Complete. *It will be helpful for you to have your Bible and a copy of the commentary available as you work through this lesson.*

Getting Started

From the Commentary

If you received a letter from a man you had never met, a man who was a prisoner, accused of being a troublemaker, how would you respond?

The Colossian believers faced that exact problem. They knew that Paul had been instrumental in leading their pastor, Epaphras, to saving faith in Christ. They also knew that Epaphras had gone to Rome to consult with Paul and had not yet returned. The church members had received Paul's letter, brought to them by Tychicus and Onesimus. But the false teachers in Colossae had been discrediting Paul and causing doubts in the people's minds. "Why listen to a man who is a political prisoner?" they asked. "Can you trust him?"

—*Be Complete,* page 71

1. How would you approach a potentially antagonistic audience with a message meant to clarify mistaken beliefs? What does it take to build trust in matters of faith and belief? What does Paul do, particularly in these verses, to address the claims that he isn't worth trusting?

2. Choose one verse or phrase from Colossians 1:21—2:3 that stands out to you. This could be something you're intrigued by, something that makes you uncomfortable, something that puzzles you, something that resonates with you, or just something you want to examine further. Write that here. What strikes you about this verse?

Going Deeper

From the Commentary

> The word translated "alienated" means "estranged." These
> Gentiles in Colossae were estranged from God and sepa-
> rated from the spiritual blessings of Israel (Eph. 2:11ff.).
> The gods that they worshipped were false gods, and their
> religious rituals could not take care of their sin or guilt.
>
> —*Be Complete*, page 72

3. How do Paul's statements in Colossians 1:23–27 build his case that he is
a trustworthy teacher of the faith? Why is this personal information about
Paul critical to his ministry toward the Colossian church?

From the Commentary

> They did not reconcile themselves to God; it was God
> who took the initiative in His love and grace. The Father
> sent the Son to die on a cross that sinners might be rec-
> onciled to God.
>
> —*Be Complete*, page 72

4. Paul makes a point to restate that it was God's action that prompted recon-ciliation (1:22). What sorts of questionable doctrines might have prompted this teaching? What is a Christian's response to people who claim that because God loves everybody, they don't need Christ's death to reconcile them to God?

More to Consider: What did Paul mean when he referred to the Colos-sian Christians as being presented "without blemish" and "free from accusation"? (See Col. 1:22.)

From Today's World

Paul comments in 2:1 that he's struggling for all those who have not met him personally. In today's Internet age, we have access to information and teaching from a variety of sources that eliminates the distance Paul had to deal with. Now, if you want to learn what a pastor in San Diego preached about last week, all you have to do is look up the church online and down-load the sermon. The same, however, is true for all kinds of teaching that is non-Christian or pseudo-Christian.

5. How important is it for Christians to have a relationship with the leaders and pastors who are teaching them? Why? What are the sorts of things one

misses out on if a teacher-student relationship is played out only via e-mails or letters and never in person?

From the Commentary

> "Instead of being ashamed of my suffering, I am rejoicing in it!" How could anyone rejoice in suffering? To begin with, Paul was suffering because of Jesus Christ. It was "the fellowship of his sufferings" (Phil. 3:10). Like the early apostles, Paul rejoiced that he was "counted worthy to suffer shame for his name" (Acts 5:41). A Christian should never suffer "as a thief, or as an evildoer," but it is an honor to "suffer as a Christian" (1 Peter 4:15–16). There is a special blessing and reward reserved for the faithful believer who suffers for the sake of Christ (Matt. 5:10–12).
>
> —*Be Complete*, page 75

6. What makes it difficult to rejoice in suffering? Why do you think Paul was able to do this?

More to Consider: Read Colossians 1:22–23. Does this statement suggest a believer can lose his or her salvation? Why or why not?

From the Commentary

Had Paul compromised with the Jews and stopped ministering to the Gentiles, he could have been spared a great deal of suffering. But he could not abandon his calling just for personal safety and comfort. He had been made a minister by God; he had been given a "stewardship" (dispensation) and he had to be faithful to his calling (1 Cor. 4:2). It was not a matter of choice: he was called to fulfill the Word of God. This can mean "I must preach the Word fully and not compromise any truth." It can also mean "I am commissioned by God's Word and I must be faithful to discharge my office."

—*Be Complete*, page 76

7. Paul's role as a minister to the Gentiles is critical to the growth of the early church. Circle or list every mention he makes of how difficult his struggle has been to do this. How might things have played out differently in early church history if he had chosen not to become the church's "servant by the commission God gave" him (1:25)?

From the Commentary

> The false teachers exalted themselves and their great "spiritual" attainments. They preached a system of teaching, but Paul preached a Person. The gnostics preached philosophy and the empty traditions of men (Col. 2:8), but Paul proclaimed Jesus Christ. The false teachers had lists of rules and regulations (Col. 2:16, 20–21), but Paul presented Christ. What a difference in ministries!
>
> —*Be Complete*, pages 78–79

8. What is "the mystery that has been kept hidden" (1:26–27; 2:2–3)? Why do you think Paul refers to a mystery? Why would this particular word resonate with the Colossian believers?

Paul also uses the word *wisdom* again in this portion of the letter. What is the difference between Paul's use of the word and the likely use of the word by the false teachers, who claimed to have greater wisdom than Paul?

From the Commentary

> [Paul] wanted to present every believer "perfect in Christ
> Jesus." The word *perfect* was a favorite word with the gnos-
> tic teachers. It described the disciple who was no longer a
> novice, but who had matured and was fully instructed in
> the secrets of the religion. Paul used it to mean "complete,
> mature in Christ."
>
> —*Be Complete*, page 79

9. Why is it significant that Paul continually uses words the gnostics
spouted? What does this teach us about how we might best relate to those
who are either preaching false doctrine or have no understanding of the
Christian message?

*More to Consider: Read Colossians 2:2. What are the evidences Paul
gives here that describe spiritual maturity? Why are these important
to believers?*

From the Commentary

> What a picture of prayer! So much of our praying is calm
> and comfortable, and yet Paul exerted his spiritual muscles
> the way a Greek runner would exert himself in the Olym-
> pic Games. He also taught Epaphras to pray the same way
> (Col. 4:12).
>
> This does not mean that our prayers are more effective if
> we exert all kinds of fleshly energy. Nor does it mean that
> we must "wrestle with God" and wear Him out before He
> will meet our needs. Paul described a *spiritual* striving: It
> was God's power at work in his life.
>
> *—Be Complete*, pages 80–81

10. Paul's mention of "struggling with all [Christ's] energy" (1:29) to pro-
claim Him is particularly powerful since Paul has known a lot of suffering
in his life up to this point. Why do you think he uses this imagery in
connection with his desire to teach the Colossians?

Looking Inward

Take a moment to reflect on all that you've explored thus far in this study of Colossians 1:21—2:3. Review your notes and answers and think about how each of these things matters in your life today.

Tips for Small Groups: To get the most out of this section, form pairs or trios and have group members take turns answering these questions. Be honest and as open as you can in this discussion, but most of all, be encouraging and supportive of others. Be sensitive to those who are going through particularly difficult times and don't press people to speak if they're uncomfortable doing so.

11. How do you determine if a teacher (or what he or she is teaching) is trustworthy? How do you build your own trustworthiness among other believers and nonbelievers? Are there areas in your life that would cause others to question your trustworthiness? If so, what are those areas, and how can you go about addressing them?

12. What does it mean to you to rejoice in suffering? Can you do this? If so, how? What makes it difficult to rejoice when things aren't going the way you'd hoped? How can Paul's story encourage you to rejoice through suffering?

13. Paul speaks of Christ as the source of wisdom and knowledge. How important to you are wisdom and knowledge (as opposed to information and entertainment)? Why is that? How does a person cultivate wisdom? How is that different from amassing information?

Going Forward

14. Think of one or two things you have learned that you'd like to focus on in the coming week. Remember that this is all about quality, not quantity. It's better to address one specific area of life and do it well than to work on many and do poorly (or to be so overwhelmed that you simply don't try).

Do you need to cultivate gratitude for the fact that you have been reconciled to God through Christ? Do you need to value the "mystery" of Christ more deeply or make wisdom a priority over information? Be specific. Go back through Colossians 1:21—2:3 and put a star next to the phrase or verse that is most encouraging to you. Consider memorizing this verse.

Real-Life Application Ideas: Spend some time online or in your local library studying pseudo-Christian cults. See what you can uncover about the similarities and differences between those cults and orthodox Christianity. What sorts of doctrines are usually twisted in cults? How well do you understand those doctrines in your own spiritual life? If you feel unsure about some of these, pursue answers through Scripture, prayer, and your church.

Seeking Help

15. Write a prayer below (or simply pray one in silence), inviting God to work on your mind and heart in those areas you've previously noted. Be honest about your desires and fears.

Notes for Small Groups:

- *Look for ways to put into practice the things you wrote in the Going Forward section in this lesson. Talk with other group members about your ideas and commit to being accountable to one another.*

- *During the coming week, ask the Holy Spirit to continue to reveal truth to you from what you've read and studied.*

- *Before you start the next lesson, read Colossians 2:4–15. For more in-depth lesson preparation, read chapter 6, "Saints Alive—and Alert," in* Be Complete.

No Deception
(COLOSSIANS 2:4–15)

Before you begin …
- *Pray for the Holy Spirit to reveal truth and wisdom as you go through this lesson.*
- *Read Colossians 2:4–15. This lesson references chapter 6 in* Be Complete. *It will be helpful for you to have your Bible and a copy of the commentary available as you work through this lesson.*

Getting Started

From the Commentary

In the Christian life, we never stand still—we either go forward or gradually slip backward. "Let us go on to maturity!" is the call we must obey (Heb. 6:1, literal translation). The Christian who is not making spiritual progress is an open target for the Enemy to attack and destroy.

—Be Complete, pages 85–86

1. Paul's first comment in this section is a bold statement. He writes, "I tell you this so that no one may deceive you by fine-sounding arguments" (Col. 2:4). Why do you think he makes such a statement?

2. Choose one verse or phrase from Colossians 2:4–15 that stands out to you. This could be something you're intrigued by, something that makes you uncomfortable, something that puzzles you, something that resonates with you, or just something you want to examine further. Write that here. What strikes you about this verse?

Going Deeper

From the Commentary

> Satan is deceptive. He wants to lead believers astray, and to do this, he uses deceptive words. The Greek term used

here describes the persuasive arguments of a lawyer. Satan is a liar (John 8:44), and by his lies he leads believers into the wrong path. It is important that we exercise spiritual discernment, and that we continue to grow in our knowledge of spiritual truth.

—*Be Complete*, page 86

3. Paul encourages the Colossians to stay on course by saying that he is "present with [them] in spirit." When we're confused about what's right and what's not, how can connections with fellow believers help? Why is it tempting to try to figure things out on our own, rather than building consistent relationships with fellow believers?

From the Commentary

The Christian life is compared to a pilgrimage, and believers must learn to walk. Paul had already encouraged his readers to "walk worthy of the Lord" (Col. 1:10), and later he used this image again (Col. 3:7; 4:5). In the Ephesian epistle, the companion letter to the Colossian epistle, Paul used the image at least seven times (Eph. 2:2, 10; 4:1, 17; 5:2, 8, 15).

—*Be Complete*, page 86

4. Paul uses the word "rooted" to describe the believer's condition (2:7). What does he mean by "rooted"? How is this imagery of particular significance for Christians facing attacks or dealing with questionable doctrine? How can a person walk (that is, keep moving) and still be rooted?

From Today's World

Many aspects of the gnostic cult that the Colossians struggled with are found today in a growing Jewish offshoot called Kabbalah. The recent surge of interest in this belief system may have been spurred in part by celebrities who are pursuing it, but also by its focus on mysticism, which has become a popular buzzword not only in Kabbalah, but also in mainstream Christianity.

5. What is it about mysticism that attracts people? Why might well-meaning Christians overlook basic tenets of faith in pursuit of mystical knowledge? How does the promise of unique or exclusive knowledge compare to the mystery that Paul writes about in Colossians?

From the Commentary

> Paul continued the military image with this warning:
> "Beware lest any man carry you off as a captive" (literal
> translation). The false teachers did not go out and win
> the lost, any more than the cultists do today. They "kid-
> napped" converts from churches! Most of the people I
> have talked with who are members of anti-Christian cults
> were at one time associated with a Christian church of one
> denomination or another.
>
> —*Be Complete*, page 88

6. Some philosophies/spiritualities get their cachet from their real or supposed connection to "human tradition" (2:8)—the ancient secrets of the
gnostics, Egyptians, Druids, Buddha, Lost Gospel of Judas, and others.
Why are such traditions appealing?

Other philosophies gain their legitimacy from association with "the
basic principles of this world" (2:8), such as quantum physics or biology,
which explain how the world works. What's the appeal with these?

From the Commentary

> This philosophy of the false teachers is "hollow and decep-
> tive" (Col. 2:8 NIV) for several reasons. To begin with, it
> is the tradition of men and not the truth of God's Word.
> The word *tradition* means "that which is handed down"; and
> there is a true Christian tradition (1 Cor. 15:3ff.; 2 Thess.
> 2:15; 3:6; 2 Tim. 2:2). The important thing about any teach-
> ing is its origin: Did it come from God or from man?
>
> —*Be Complete*, page 88

7. Tradition is important to Christianity. What are some examples of traditions that are "from man"? What are some examples that come from God?
Are traditions from humans universally bad? Why or why not?

From the Commentary

> Paul made it clear that the Christian is not subject in any
> way to the Old Testament legal system, *nor can it do him
> any good spiritually*. Jesus Christ *alone* is sufficient for our
> every spiritual need, for all of God's fullness is in Him. We

are identified with Jesus Christ because He is the Head of
the body (Col. 1:18) and we are the members of the body
(1 Cor. 12:12–13).

—*Be Complete*, page 92

8. Paul uses the example of circumcision to explain why Christians are no
longer subject to the laws of the Old Testament. How might the Gentile
believers have responded to this explanation?

*More to Consider: Paul compares Christians with Jews in 2:11. What
is this comparison? How might the Colossian Christians have received
this? What are the implications of this truth today?*

From the Commentary

Keep in mind that in the New Testament, the word *bap-
tize* has both a literal and a figurative meaning. The literal
meaning is "to dip, to immerse." The figurative meaning
is "to be identified with." …

Paul used the word *baptism* in a figurative sense in this section of his letter—for no amount of material water could bury a person with Christ or make him alive in Christ.

—*Be Complete*, page 93

9. What does baptism represent? How does baptism declare the preeminence of Christ? Why do you think Paul mentions baptism in this passage?

More to Consider: Read 1 Peter 2:24. How does this passage support Paul's message about the law in Colossians 2:14?

From the Commentary

Jesus not only dealt with sin and the law on the cross, but He also dealt with Satan. Speaking about His crucifixion, Jesus said, "Now is the judgment of this world; now shall the prince of this world be cast out" (John 12:31). The death of Christ on the cross looked like a great victory for

Satan, but it turned out to be a great defeat from which
Satan cannot recover.

—Be Complete, page 95

10. In 2:15, Paul makes a bold statement about Christ's disarming of the
"powers and authorities." Why is it important for us to know that the
"powers and authorities" have been disarmed?

Looking Inward

Take a moment to reflect on all that you've explored thus far in this study
of Colossians 2:4–15. Review your notes and answers and think about how
each of these things matters in your life today.

> *Tips for Small Groups: To get the most out of this section, form pairs
> or trios and have group members take turns answering these ques-
> tions. Be honest and as open as you can in this discussion, but most of
> all, be encouraging and supportive of others. Be sensitive to those who
> are going through particularly difficult times and don't press people to
> speak if they're uncomfortable doing so.*

11. What are some ways you have been deceived about doctrinal issues? How did that deception affect the practical living of your faith? What are some areas today where Satan is attempting to deceive you? How will you go about dealing with these things?

12. What aspects of mysticism appeal to you? How does Paul's idea of growth through suffering compare with the pain-free life promised by some false doctrines? In what ways are you tempted to seek whatever "truth" will help you avoid pain?

13. Have you ever followed the traditions of humankind at the expense of the traditions that come from God? Explain. How do you determine the right thing to do in those circumstances? What are some areas of your life today that might need reevaluation concerning the traditions you follow?

Going Forward

14. Think of one or two things you have learned that you'd like to focus on in the coming week. Remember that this is all about quality, not quantity. It's better to address one specific area of life and do it well than to work on many and do poorly (or to be so overwhelmed that you simply don't try).

Do you need to learn more about mysticism and the biblical understanding of wisdom? Do you need to evaluate traditions to make sure you're following God's Word instead of humankind's? Be specific. Go back through Colossians 2:4–15 and put a star next to the phrase or verse that is most encouraging to you. Consider memorizing this verse.

Real-Life Application Ideas: If you have been baptized, take a few moments to reflect on that experience and how it identified you with Christ. What does it mean to you to be identified with Christ? How is that different from following a set of rules (as in the Old Testament)? Make a plan to talk with someone who hasn't yet been baptized about that experience. And if you haven't yet been baptized, talk with a pastor or trusted leader about what it means to see if you're ready to take that step.

Seeking Help

15. Write a prayer below (or simply pray one in silence), inviting God to work on your mind and heart in those areas you've previously noted. Be honest about your desires and fears.

Notes for Small Groups:
- *Look for ways to put into practice the things you wrote in the Going Forward section in this lesson. Talk with other group members about your ideas and commit to being accountable to one another.*
- *During the coming week, ask the Holy Spirit to continue to reveal truth to you from what you've read and studied.*
- *Before you start the next lesson, read Colossians 2:16–23. For more in-depth lesson preparation, read chapter 7, "Believer, Beware!" in* Be Complete.

No Legalism
(COLOSSIANS 2:16–23)

Before you begin ...
- *Pray for the Holy Spirit to reveal truth and wisdom as you go through this lesson.*
- *Read Colossians 2:16–23. This lesson references chapter 7 in* Be Complete. *It will be helpful for you to have your Bible and a copy of the commentary available as you work through this lesson.*

Getting Started

From the Commentary

Paul had already warned about the false teachers (Col. 2:8). In this section of his letter, Paul gave three warnings for us to heed if we are to enjoy our fullness in Jesus Christ.

—*Be Complete,* page 99

1. What are the three warnings Paul gives us in Colossians 2:16–23? Why are these of particular importance to the Colossian Christians? Why are they important for Christians today?

More to Consider: The believing Gentiles in Colossae were never under the law of Moses. Why do you think they were tempted to submit themselves to it? What might have prompted that sort of thinking? In what ways do Christians today look for a system of rules to follow?

2. Choose one verse or phrase from Colossians 2:16–23 that stands out to you. This could be something you're intrigued by, something that makes you uncomfortable, something that puzzles you, something that resonates with you, or just something you want to examine further. Write that here. What strikes you about this verse?

Going Deeper

From the Commentary

> This warning [Let no one judge you (Col. 2:16–17)] exposes the danger of the *legalism* of the gnostic teachers in Colossae. Their doctrines were a strange mixture of Eastern mysticism, Jewish legalism, and a smattering of philosophy and Christian teaching.
>
> —*Be Complete*, page 99

3. The Colossians were primarily Gentiles unschooled in the Jewish law. For them the Jewish system was a novelty, but also intriguing because it was ancient. What is appealing about a smorgasbord approach to religion? How do people do this today?

From the Commentary

> The law is but a shadow; but in Christ we have the reality, the substance. "The law is only a shadow of the good things that are coming" (Heb. 10:1 NIV). Why go back into shadows when we have the reality in Jesus

Christ? This is like trying to hug a shadow when the reality is at hand!

—*Be Complete*, page 102

4. The kosher-food laws, festivals, and other features of Jewish law were useful for centuries, says Paul, but "these are a shadow of the things that were to come" (2:17). In what sense did they foreshadow the real thing: Christ?

From Today's World

Paul's words in this section of Colossians resonate as loudly today as they did when the Colossians were struggling with false doctrines. From one church to the next, even one Christian to the next, people today are in a constant struggle both with the legalism Paul chastises and with the world-liness he speaks against. In some churches today, the message is summed up in one word: *grace*. Of course, this is the message of Christ, but imma-ture Christians may interpret this as "license to sin." Meanwhile, other churches preach a list of dos and don'ts that might as well have come from the mouths of Pharisees.

5. What are the "principles of this world" (2:20) that Christians are struggling with today? What might Paul have to say to today's churches regarding
legalism? Grace? Responsibility?

From the Commentary

> The word translated "beguile" in the King James Version
> means "to declare unworthy of a prize." It is an athletic
> term: The umpire disqualifies the contestant because he
> has not obeyed the rules. The contestant does not cease
> to be a citizen of the land, but he forfeits the honor of
> winning a prize. A Christian who fails to obey God's
> directions does not lose his salvation. But he does lose the
> approval of the Lord and the rewards He has promised to
> those who are faithful (1 Cor. 3:8).
>
> —*Be Complete*, page 102

6. What does it mean to be disqualified from the prize (2:18)? What is the
"prize" Paul is referring to?

From the Commentary

> Trying to reach God the Father through anyone or any-
> thing other than His Son, Jesus Christ, is idolatry. Jesus
> Christ is the one and only Mediator between God and
> man (John 14:6; 1 Tim. 2:5). The person who worships
> through angels or saints now in heaven does not prove his
> humility, for he is not submitting to the authority of God's
> Word. Actually, he reveals a subtle kind of pride that sub-
> stitutes man-made traditions for the Word of God.
>
> —*Be Complete*, page 104

7. What is the false humility Paul writes about? Where is this found in today's church? How would Paul advise us to deal with it?

From the Commentary

> It is possible to be *in* a local church and not draw on the
> Head and the nourishment of the spiritual body. The false
> teachers in Colossae sought to introduce their teachings
> into the local assembly, and if they succeeded, they would

have caused the spiritual nourishment to *decrease* instead of *increase*. Unless the members of the local assembly abide in Christ, yield to the Spirit, and obey the Word, they cannot experience the life of the Head, Jesus Christ.

—*Be Complete*, pages 105–6

8. Circle phrases in 2:20–23 that suggest some of the false teachings being presented to the Colossian Christians. What does Paul say about these practices? What gives them "an appearance of wisdom" (v. 23)?

More to Consider: Read Mark 7:18–19 and Romans 14:14. How do these passages speak to Paul's reasoning about the role of food in Colossians 2:22? What are similar issues Christians wrestle with today?

From the Commentary

The people who practice asceticism have a "reputation" for spirituality, but the product does not live up to the promotion. I am amazed at the way educated people in America flock to see and hear gurus and other Eastern spiritual leaders whose teachings cannot change the human heart. This "self-imposed worship" is not the true worship of God, which must be "in spirit and in truth" (John 4:24). Their humility is false, and their harsh disciplines accomplish nothing for the inner man.

—*Be Complete*, page 108

9. What is asceticism? How is it practiced today? What's the difference between unhelpful asceticism and good bodily disciplines?

From the Commentary

The answer to legalism is the spiritual reality we have in Christ. The answer to mysticism is the spiritual union with Christ, the Head of the church. The answer to asceticism is our position in Christ in death, burial, and resurrection.

—*Be Complete*, page 109

10. Respond to each of Wiersbe's conclusions in the previous excerpt. How do these play out practically in the life of a believer?

Looking Inward

Take a moment to reflect on all that you've explored thus far in this study of Colossians 2:16–23. Review your notes and answers and think about how each of these things matters in your life today.

Tips for Small Groups: To get the most out of this section, form pairs or trios and have group members take turns answering these questions. Be honest and as open as you can in this discussion, but most of all, be encouraging and supportive of others. Be sensitive to those who are going through particularly difficult times and don't press people to speak if they're uncomfortable doing so.

11. In what ways are you tempted to be legalistic in your expression of faith? How do you draw the line between responsible actions and legalistic actions? If you tend toward legalism, what are some good ways to fight that tendency?

12. Have you ever felt as if you'd been disqualified from the prize because of something you'd done? If so, what prompted that feeling? Nothing you've done can permanently disqualify you from God's embrace. If you have confessed it, He has forgiven it. What are steps you can take to build confidence in your right standing with Christ?

13. How have you experienced or witnessed false humility? What prompts that way of thinking and acting? Why are we so concerned about the way others view us? What would it look like in your life for you to let go of those things in pursuit of a greater maturity of faith? What sorts of things would you have to let go in order to get over the tyranny of other people's approval?

Going Forward

14. Think of one or two things you have learned that you'd like to focus on in the coming week. Remember that this is all about quality, not quantity. It's better to address one specific area of life and do it well than to work on many and do poorly (or to be so overwhelmed that you simply don't try).

Do you need to examine your legalistic tendencies? Do you need to confront the ways you're tyrannized by what other people think? Be specific. Go back through Colossians 2:16–23 and put a star next to the phrase or verse that is most encouraging to you. Consider memorizing this verse.

Real-Life Application Ideas: Invite your small-group leader or a pastor who knows you well to lunch to do a bit of analysis concerning your legalistic tendencies. Ask for an honest, unfiltered examination of his or her observations. Then discuss ways to grow maturity in that area of your Christian walk.

Seeking Help

15. Write a prayer below (or simply pray one in silence), inviting God to work on your mind and heart in those areas you've previously noted. Be honest about your desires and fears.

Notes for Small Groups:
- *Look for ways to put into practice the things you wrote in the Going Forward section in this lesson. Talk with other group members about your ideas and commit to being accountable to one another.*
- *During the coming week, ask the Holy Spirit to continue to reveal truth to you from what you've read and studied.*
- *Before you start the next lesson, read Colossians 3:1–17. For more in-depth lesson preparation, read chapters 8 and 9, "Heaven on Earth" and "All Dressed Up and Someplace to Go," in* Be Complete.

Clean Clothes
(COLOSSIANS 3:1–17)

Before you begin ...
- *Pray for the Holy Spirit to reveal truth and wisdom as you go through this lesson.*
- *Read Colossians 3:1–17. This lesson references chapters 8 and 9 in* Be Complete. *It will be helpful for you to have your Bible and a copy of the commentary available as you work through this lesson.*

Getting Started
From the Commentary

In the final two chapters of Colossians, Paul moved into the practical application of the doctrines he had been teaching. After all, it does little good if Christians *declare* and *defend* the truth, but fail to *demonstrate* it in their lives.

—Be Complete, *page 113*

1. Notice that Paul opens this section with the word "Since" (v. 1). What is the significance of that word choice? Why is it of key importance to the Colossian Christians in particular? Why is it important for us today?

2. Choose one verse or phrase from Colossians 3:1–17 that stands out to you. This could be something you're intrigued by, something that makes you uncomfortable, something that puzzles you, something that resonates with you, or just something you want to examine further. Write that here. What strikes you about this verse?

Going Deeper

From the Commentary

> The emphasis [in Colossians 3:1–4] is on the believer's relationship with Christ:

We died with Christ (v. 3a).

We live in Christ (v. 4a).

We are raised with Christ (v. 1a).

We are hidden in Christ (v. 3b).

We are glorified in Christ (v. 4b).

—*Be Complete*, pages 114–15

3. Colossians 3:1–4 is a further clarification of Christ's role in the believer's life. Why do you think Paul chose to explain this in more detail to the Colossian Christians? What are the practical implications nested in these words?

From the Commentary

The word *mortify* means "put to death." Because we have died with Christ (Col. 3:3), we have the spiritual power to slay the earthly, fleshly desires that want to control us. Paul called this "reckoning" ourselves to be dead to sin but alive in Christ (Rom. 6:11). Our Lord used the same idea when He said, "And if thy right eye offend thee, pluck it out" (Matt. 5:29–30).

—*Be Complete*, page 117

4. Paul often uses this image of "putting to death" those things that are of the former life (vv. 3, 5). What are some false teachings and practices that believers today need to put to death?

From the History Books

The Essenes were a Jewish sect that flourished between the second century BC and the first century AD. To become a member of this group, one had to take an oath that included practicing piety toward God, maintaining a pure lifestyle, and abstaining from immoral activities. It was their intent to live according to a strict set of rules, in sharp contrast to the Jews they referred to as the "breakers of the covenant." While some might argue that their rigid adherence to rules was simply another form of impossible legalism, they are credited with having preserved some of our earliest manuscripts of the Bible, commonly referred to as the Dead Sea Scrolls.

5. While Paul rejects legalism, he follows that up with practical (and very Jewish) instructions about avoiding sexual immorality, impurity, and so on.

How do these two teachings line up? What makes asceticism misguided and these other practical behaviors right? How does the word "Since" that Paul uses to open the section play into this argument?

More to Consider: Why do you think Paul adds "covetousness" to his list of sensual sins in Colossians 3:5–9 (KJV)? (Remember "You shall not covet" is one of the Ten Commandments. See Ex. 20:17.)

From the Commentary

After warning us against the sensual sins, Paul then pointed out the dangers of the social sins (Col. 3:8–9). Dr. G. Campbell Morgan called these "the sins in good standing." We are so accustomed to anger, critical attitudes, lying, and coarse humor among believers that we are no longer upset or convicted about these sins. We would be shocked to see a church member commit some sensual sin, but we will watch him lose his temper in a business meeting and call it "righteous indignation."

—*Be Complete*, page 119

6. Why do you think Paul makes a point to describe not only the sensual sins, but the social ones as well? What are examples of these social sins in the church today? Why do you think our culture tends to be more concerned with sensual sins? Is this appropriate? Why or why not?

More to Consider: The Greeks had two different words for new. *The word* neos *meant "new in time." We use this word as an English prefix in such words as* neoorthodoxy *and* neoclassicism. *The word* kainos *meant "new in quality, fresh." Sometimes the two words were used interchangeably in the New Testament, but there still is a fundamental difference. Which of these meanings best fits Paul's description of the "new self" in Colossians 3:10? How might each of these words apply?*

From the Commentary

The word *elect* means "chosen of God." God's words to Israel through Moses help us to understand the meaning of salvation by grace: "The LORD did not set his love upon you, nor choose you, because ye were more in number than any people; for ye were the fewest of all people. But because the LORD loved you … hath the LORD brought you out [of Egypt] with a mighty hand" (Deut. 7:7–8).

This miracle of divine election did not depend on anything that we are or that we have done, for God chose us in Christ "before the foundation of the world" (Eph. 1:4). If God saved a sinner on the basis of merit or works, nobody would be saved. It is all done through God's grace that it might all bring glory to God.

—*Be Complete*, pages 127–28

7. Why is the concept of being "chosen" critical to Paul's teaching in 3:12–14? If we're not chosen by merit, then why does it matter if we're compassionate, patient people?

From the Commentary

Chosen by God, set apart for God, loved by God, and forgiven by God. They all add up to GRACE! … Paul named eight graces:

1. Put on … tender mercies (Col. 3:12).

2. Put on … kindness (Col. 3:12).

3. Put on … humbleness of mind (Col. 3:12).

4. Put on … meekness (Col. 3:12).

5. Put on … longsuffering (Col. 3:12).

6. Put on … forbearance (Col. 3:13).

7. Put on … forgiveness (Col. 3:13).

8. Put on … love (Col. 3:14).

—Be Complete, pages 129–31

8. In your Bible, circle the graces Paul lists (as noted by Wiersbe in the *Be Complete* excerpt). Why are they graces and not tasks to accomplish? How, in practice, does a person put on these graces? In what ways is this action of putting on graces different from following legalistic rules?

From the Commentary

When a Christian loses the peace of God, he begins to go off in directions that are out of the will of God. He turns to the things of the world and the flesh to compensate for his lack of peace within. He tries to escape, but he cannot escape *himself!* It is only when he confesses his sin, claims God's forgiveness, and does God's will that he experiences God's peace within.

When there is peace in the heart, there will be praise on the lips: "And be ye thankful" (Col. 3:15). The Christian out of God's will is never found giving sincere praise to God.

—*Be Complete*, page 132

9. Paul encourages readers to "let the peace of Christ" rule in their hearts. In what ways do we allow or not allow Christ to rule in our hearts? How is this different from chasing peace? What role does the Holy Spirit play in giving us this peace?

From the Commentary

Paul described a local church worship service (1 Cor. 14:26; Col. 3:16). Note that the believer sings to *himself* as well as to the other believers and to the Lord. Our singing must be from our hearts and not just our lips. But if the Word of

God is not in our hearts, we cannot sing from our hearts.
This shows how important it is to know the Word of God,
for it enriches our public and private worship of God.

—*Be Complete*, page 134

10. How does Paul's description of a church service in verse 16 compare to your church experience? What clues does he give about the practices and purpose of church? What can today's church learn from this passage?

Looking Inward

Take a moment to reflect on all that you've explored thus far in this study of Colossians 3:1–17. Review your notes and answers and think about how each of these things matters in your life today.

> *Tips for Small Groups: To get the most out of this section, form pairs or trios and have group members take turns answering these questions. Be honest and as open as you can in this discussion, but most of all, be encouraging and supportive of others. Be sensitive to those who are going through particularly difficult times and don't press for people to speak if they're uncomfortable doing so.*

11. Consider Paul's teaching on the believer's relationship with Christ in 3:1–4. Which of these aspects is easiest for you to understand? Which is the most difficult? How can you grow in your understanding of what it means to be "in Christ" according to Paul's message?

12. What appeals to you about the idea of putting to death the things of the world? What makes that difficult in actual practice? Think about areas in your life where you're still pursuing earthly pleasures. How might you go about setting your heart on "things above" instead? What practical steps can you take toward this end?

13. What does it mean to you that you have been "chosen" by God? How does that affect your daily living (if at all)?

Going Forward

14. Think of one or two things you have learned that you'd like to work on in the coming week. Remember that this is all about quality, not quantity. It's better to work on one specific area of life and do it well than to work on many and do poorly (or to be so overwhelmed that you simply don't try).

Do you need to put to death areas of sin in your life? Do you need to better understand what it means to have been "raised with Christ"? Be specific. Go back through Colossians 3:1–17 and put a star next to the phrase or verse that is most encouraging to you. Consider memorizing this verse.

Real-Life Application Ideas: Take stock of your social sins this week to see how well you're living out the life Jesus has called you into. Before you begin this exercise, discuss the idea of "social sins" with a friend to determine what sorts of things might qualify. Then consider having him or her hold you accountable to seriously examining your behaviors at work, at home, or in your community. You might discover areas in your life that you might want to change by putting on the clothes of compassion, kindness, humility, gentleness, and patience (Col. 3:12).

Seeking Help

15. Write a prayer below (or simply pray one in silence), inviting God to work on your mind and heart in those areas you've previously noted. Be honest about your desires and fears.

Notes for Small Groups:

- *Look for ways to put into practice the things you wrote in the Going Forward section in this lesson. Talk with other group members about your ideas and commit to being accountable to one another.*

- *During the coming week, ask the Holy Spirit to continue to reveal truth to you from what you've read and studied.*

- *Before you start the next lesson, read Colossians 3:18—4:1. For more in-depth lesson preparation, read chapter 10, "A Family Affair," in* Be Complete.

Family Matters

(COLOSSIANS 3:18—4:1)

Before you begin ...
* *Pray for the Holy Spirit to reveal truth and wisdom as*
   you go through this lesson.
* *Read Colossians 3:18—4:1. This lesson references chapter*
   10 in Be Complete. *It will be helpful for you to have*
   your Bible and a copy of the commentary available as
   you work through this lesson.

Getting Started

From the Commentary

Faith in Jesus Christ not only changes individuals; it also
changes homes. In this section, Paul addressed himself
to family members: husbands and wives, children, and
household servants. It seems clear that these persons being
addressed were believers since the apostle appealed to all
of them to live to please Jesus Christ.

—*Be Complete,* page 139

1. Why does Paul turn his attention to families in this section of Colossians? How might the threat of false doctrines have influenced his decision to discuss the roles of family members?

2. Choose one verse or phrase from Colossians 3:18—4:1 that stands out to you. This could be something you're intrigued by, something that makes you uncomfortable, something that puzzles you, something that resonates with you, or just something you want to examine further. Write that here. What strikes you about this verse?

Going Deeper

From the Commentary

> We must not think of *submission* as "slavery" or "subjuga-
> tion." The word comes from the military vocabulary and
> simply means "to arrange under rank." The fact that one
> soldier is a private and another is a colonel does not mean
> that one man is necessarily *better* than the other. It only
> means that they have different ranks.
>
> —*Be Complete*, page 140

3. Verse 18 speaks to a controversial topic in Christian circles: submission.
As you read this statement in context, do you see submission as controversial? Why or why not? What makes the idea of submission contentious to
Christians and non-Christians alike? What would be another way to say
what Paul is saying without using the word *submission*?

From the Commentary

> Headship is not dictatorship or lordship. It is loving lead-
> ership. In fact, both the husband and the wife must be
> submitted to the *Lord* and to *each other* (Eph. 5:21). It is a
> mutual respect under the lordship of Jesus Christ.
>
> —*Be Complete*, page 140

4. What does it look like when both the husband and the wife are submitted
to the Lord? How does that provide the framework for loving leadership as
described in Colossians 3:19? Why is it important for someone to be the head
of the marriage? Does this challenge the idea of equality? Why or why not?

From Today's World

The family of today is often much different than that of even twenty-five
years ago. The traditional roles of husband as breadwinner and wife as home-
maker have long been replaced by working moms and stay-at-home dads
and two-income families and a host of other variations. While many families still strive for regular family times such as eating together and spending
time together playing or learning, the once-clear roles for mom and dad
have become fuzzy for many.

5. As you consider Paul's admonitions for husbands and wives in 3:18–19, do you think they still apply even when the roles are altered in day-to-day living? What, if any, adjustments or additions might Paul make in his treatise were he to see the differing roles in the households across the world today?

More to Consider: Happy marriages don't come automatically. They require work. Go back through Colossians 3:5–14 and review the "grace clothes" Paul talks about. How do these characteristics help a husband and wife build a happy marriage? Is this easy? What sorts of sacrifices must each make to build a strong marriage?

From the Commentary

Children have rights, but they also have responsibilities, and their foremost responsibility is to obey. They are to obey "in all things" and not simply in those things that please them. Will their parents ever ask them to do something that is wrong? Not if the parents are submitted to the Lord and to one another, and not if they love each other and their children.

The child who does not learn to obey his parents is not likely to grow up obeying *any* authority.

—*Be Complete*, page 143

6. In verse 20, Paul reminds children to obey their parents "in everything." How do you think Paul means children to understand and apply this? For instance, what if the parents aren't submitting to the Lord? What if children think the parents are making a serious mistake? Why do you think Paul chose to speak to children at all in this letter? In what ways might verses 20–21 have given children a voice they otherwise would not have had?

More to Consider: If a home is truly Christian, it is a place of encouragement (v. 21). What would Paul say makes a home truly Christian? How does that sort of environment provide encouragement for children?

From the Commentary

Slavery was an established institution in Paul's day. There were sixty million people in the Roman Empire, and many of them were well-educated people who carried great responsibilities in the homes of the wealthy. In many homes, the slaves helped to educate and discipline the children.

Why didn't the church of that day openly oppose slavery and seek to destroy it? For one thing, the church was a minority group that had no political power to change an institution that was built into the social order. Paul was careful to instruct Christian slaves to secure their freedom if they could (1 Cor. 7:21), but he did not advocate rebellion or the overthrow of the existing order.

—*Be Complete*, page 145

7. In some ways, Paul's admonition to slaves could be considered a definition of integrity. How might his teaching about obeying "not only when [the master's] eye is on you" apply to other relationships with a boss? A family member? A friend? How would things look different in your world if you and the people around you did everything as if "it is the Lord Christ you are serving"?

From the Commentary

> A Christian servant owed complete obedience to his mas-
> ter as a ministry to the Lord. If a Christian servant had a
> believing master, that servant was not to take advantage of
> his master because they were brothers in the Lord. If any-
> thing, the servant strived to do a better job because he was
> a Christian. He showed singleness of heart and gave his
> full devotion to his master. His work was done heartily,
> not grudgingly, and as to the Lord and not to men. "Ye
> serve the Lord Christ" (Col. 3:24).
>
> —*Be Complete*, page 146

8. What does "singleness of heart" look like in the workplace? How can this
sort of approach to work affect the lives of our coworkers? Supervisors? In
what other ways does a believer's intent to do everything heartily influence
the people around him or her?

*More to Consider: Read Acts 10:34; Romans 2:11; Ephesians 6:9;
and James 2:1, 9. What do these verses tell us about how God deals*

with all people, servants or rulers? What implications does this have for us today?

From the Commentary

> As we review this very practical section of Colossians, we see once again the preeminence of Jesus Christ in our lives as believers. Christ must be the Head of the home. This series of admonitions is actually a practical application of Colossians 3:17: "And whatsoever ye do in word or deed, do all in the name of the Lord Jesus." It is by His power and authority that we should live in our daily relationships. If He is the preeminent One in our lives, then we will love each other, submit to each other, obey, and treat one another fairly in the Lord.
>
> —*Be Complete*, page 148

9. Go through this section again (Col. 3:18—4:1) and consider how each of these teachings supports the concept of Christ's preeminence. Describe that connection.

From the Commentary

> The fullness of the Spirit and the fullness of the Word are needed in the home. If family members are controlled by the Spirit of God and the Word of God, they will be joyful, thankful, and submissive—and they will have little trouble getting along with each other. Christian employers and employees will treat each other fairly if they are filled with the Spirit and the Word.
>
> —*Be Complete*, page 148

10. In many ways, this "fullness" theme is a fitting summary response to the false teachers, who taught only a portion of the truth. How do we pursue the "fullness of the Spirit and the fullness of the Word"? What are practical ways to grow in Christian maturity as Paul encourages throughout Colossians?

Looking Inward

Take a moment to reflect on all that you've explored thus far in this study of Colossians 3:18—4:1. Review your notes and answers and think about how each of these things matters in your life today.

Tips for Small Groups: To get the most out of this section, form pairs or trios and have group members take turns answering these questions. Be honest and as open as you can in this discussion, but most of all, be encouraging and supportive of others. Be sensitive to those who are going through particularly difficult times and don't press for people to speak if they're uncomfortable doing so.

11. What is your reaction to Paul's admonition to wives and husbands? What does it mean to you that wives are to "submit" to their husbands? What does it mean to you that Paul admonishes husbands to "not be harsh with them"? If you're married, how do you and your spouse handle this passage of Scripture?

12. How do Paul's words about parents and children compare to your actions as a child? As a parent? What are some things you want to do better as a parent? How will you take steps toward doing these things?

13. In what ways do you exemplify integrity in the workplace? At home? If you are not living up to the standards you believe God would want you to, what are some things you can do to put off the old self in the area of parenting or submitting to authority?

Going Forward

14. Think of one or two things you have learned that you'd like to work on in the coming week. Remember that this is all about quality, not quantity. It's better to work on one specific area of life and do it well than to work on many and do poorly (or to be so overwhelmed that you simply don't try).

Do you need to evaluate your role in marriage? Consider how to better parent your children? Be specific. Go back through Colossians 3:18—4:1 and put a star next to the phrase or verse that is most encouraging to you. Consider memorizing this verse.

Real-Life Application Ideas: If you're married, make a date with your spouse to explore what the Bible says about marriage (including this passage in Colossians 3). Prayerfully consider what Paul intended in these words as well as what the Holy Spirit is saying to you about your own situation. You might also want to consider attending a respected marriage seminar to further explore your roles in relationship and to learn how to love each other better.

Seeking Help

15. Write a prayer below (or simply pray one in silence), inviting God to work on your mind and heart in those areas you've previously noted. Be honest about your desires and fears.

Notes for Small Groups:

- *Look for ways to put into practice the things you wrote in the Going Forward section in this lesson. Talk with other group members about your ideas and commit to being accountable to one another.*

- *During the coming week, ask the Holy Spirit to continue to reveal truth to you from what you've read and studied.*

- *Before you start the next lesson, read Colossians 4:2–18. For more in-depth lesson preparation, read chapters 11 and 12, "Talk Is Not Cheap!" and "Friends, Romans, Countrymen," in* Be Complete.

The Power of Words
(COLOSSIANS 4:2–18)

Before you begin ...
- *Pray for the Holy Spirit to reveal truth and wisdom as you go through this lesson.*
- *Read Colossians 4:2–18. This lesson references chapters 11 and 12 in* Be Complete. *It will be helpful for you to have your Bible and a copy of the commentary available as you work through this lesson.*

Getting Started

From the Commentary

Prayer and worship are perhaps the highest uses of the gift of speech. Paul was not ashamed to ask his friends to pray for him. Even though he was an apostle, he needed prayer support for himself and his ministry. If a great Christian like Paul felt the need for prayer support, how much more do you and I need this kind of spiritual help!

—*Be Complete*, pages 151–52

1. Review Colossians 4:2–6. How does this section of Paul's letter mirror the opening section? How would Paul's request for prayers have helped the Colossians to understand the role of prayer in spiritual maturity?

More to Consider: Review Colossians 4:2–3. Then circle these characteristics of a satisfying and spiritual prayer life Paul describes: It must be faithful; it must be watchful; it must be thankful; and it must be purposeful. How do each of these characteristics make prayer satisfying? How do you see these in evidence in the prayer life of your small group or church?

2. Choose one verse or phrase from Colossians 4:2–18 that stands out to you. This could be something you're intrigued by, something that makes you uncomfortable, something that puzzles you, something that resonates with you, or just something you want to examine further. Write that here. What strikes you about this verse?

Going Deeper

From the Commentary

> Paul did not ask for the prison doors to be opened, but
> that doors of ministry might be opened (1 Cor. 16:9; Acts
> 14:27). It was more important to Paul that he be a faithful
> minister than a free man. It is worth noting that in all of
> Paul's prison prayers, his concern was not for personal safety
> or material help, but for spiritual character and blessing.
>
> —*Be Complete*, page 154

3. Paul's prayer that "God may open a door for our message" (Col. 4:3) says a
lot about his own spiritual maturity. How would this prayer have helped the
Colossians themselves to hear his message? What does Paul's passion for being
a faithful minister, despite his circumstances, say to Christians today?

From the Commentary

> As Christians, we must never have a sanctified superiority
> complex. We have a responsibility to witness to the lost
> around us and to seek to bring them into God's family.

To begin with, we have the responsibility to *walk wisely* (Col. 4:5). *Walk* refers, of course, to our conduct in daily life. The unsaved outsiders watch us Christians and are very critical of us. There must be nothing in our lives that would jeopardize our testimony.

—*Be Complete*, page 156

4. What would it have meant to the Colossians to "walk wisely" in light of the false doctrines that threatened their congregation? What does "walking wisely" look like today? What are the threats your church or small group faces that demand graceful, salt-seasoned responses?

From the History Books

The Roman society in which Paul worked and moved was generally tolerant of religion but distrusted Christianity, which it thought of more as a superstition than a religion. Paul's imprisonment, however, came about because of a clash not with the Romans but with the Jewish leaders. The Roman government wasn't quick to judge him, but the Jewish leaders wanted him dead.

5. Paul's encouragement to the Colossians to give grace (v. 6) is particularly powerful considering his circumstances. What do you think Paul wanted

the Colossians to learn from hearing this from a man in prison? Do you think it's significant that Paul mentions his "chains" in this section of the letter? Why or why not?

From the Commentary

Our speech is supposed to "minister grace unto the hearers" (Eph. 4:29). But it cannot do that unless we have grace in our hearts and in our words. "Speaking the truth in love" (Eph. 4:15) is God's ideal for our conversation.

—*Be Complete*, page 158

6. Why did Paul add "seasoned with salt" in Colossians 4:6? How was salt used in biblical times (and also today)? What does a "salt seasoned" conversation look like in contrast to one that is not seasoned? What are some examples of salt-seasoned conversations you've observed?

From the Commentary

> Paul did not spell out the details of his personal situation
> in this letter. He left it to his two spiritual brothers, Tychi-
> cus and Onesimus, to share the burdens with the church
> in Colossae. This is another wonderful ministry of speech:
> We can share our needs and burdens with others; then
> they can encourage and assist us.
>
> —*Be Complete*, pages 158–59

7. Why do you think Paul left it in the hands of Tychicus to deliver the
news about him to the church (Col. 4:7)? What does this teach us about
the value of entrusting a friend with news? About the value of sharing each
other's burdens?

From the Commentary

> It was customary in Paul's day to close each letter with
> personal greetings. Friends did not see one another that
> much, and letter service was very slow and limited....
>
> When we first read this list of names, we are probably not
> greatly moved. But when we get behind the scenes and

discover the drama of these men's lives as they worked
with Paul, the list becomes very exciting.

—*Be Complete*, page 163

8. What strikes you as most important in Paul's closing remarks? What
do you imagine are the "stories behind the names"? How does this section of Colossians speak to the importance of community and building
friendships?

More to Consider: Review all of the names in Colossians 4:10–18.
What sorts of personal characteristics can you intuit about each from
Paul's greetings? What does this say about Paul? About his friends?

From the Commentary

We met Epaphras at the beginning of this study, for he was
the man who founded the church in Colossae (Col. 1:7–8).
He had been led to Christ through Paul's ministry in Ephesus,
and had returned home to share the good news of salvation.
It seems likely that Epaphras also founded the churches in

Laodicea and Hierapolis (Col. 4:13). In our modern terms, Epaphras became a "home missionary."

One of the secrets of the ministry of Epaphras was his prayer life.… He prayed constantly; he prayed fervently; he prayed personally; he prayed definitely; and he prayed sacrificially.

—*Be Complete*, pages 167–69

9. Why do you think Paul takes time to note that Epaphras is "always wrestling in prayer" for the Colossian church (4:12)? How would Paul's mention of Epaphras's concern and love for the church he founded have helped them in their current crisis?

From the Commentary

Paul's last words before his salutation are directed at Archippus as an encouragement to continue faithfully in his ministry. Was Archippus discouraged? Had the gnostic false teachers invaded his church and created problems for him? We do not know. But we do know that pastors of local churches face many problems and carry many burdens, and they often need a word of encouragement.

—*Be Complete*, page 172

10. What did Paul say to Archippus to encourage him (4:17)? What "work" do you think Archippus needed to complete? What sort of similar words would encourage the work of your church or small group? In what ways are Paul's words to Archippus (and his other friends) words that can be applied to the leaders of your church?

Looking Inward

Take a moment to reflect on all that you've explored thus far in this study of Colossians 4:2–18. Review your notes and answers and think about how each of these things matters in your life today.

Tips for Small Groups: To get the most out of this section, form pairs or trios and have group members take turns answering these questions. Be honest and as open as you can in this discussion, but most of all, be encouraging and supportive of others. Be sensitive to those who are going through particularly difficult times and don't press for people to speak if they're uncomfortable doing so.

11. How well do you devote yourself to prayer? What are some ways you might work at improving your prayer life? What does it mean to you

to be "watchful and thankful"? How can you apply this to your daily prayer life?

12. In what ways do you season your conversations with salt when speaking to family, friends, coworkers, and strangers? Is it always easy to do? Why or why not? What are the benefits of offering grace to those you engage in conversation? If you've spoken ungracefully, what were the results? How might you have better dealt with that circumstance?

13. Think of the friends who've had a positive impact on your faith life. How well have you communicated your thankfulness to them? What are some things you could do today to express your gratitude? Why is expressing your gratitude important to them? To you? To God?

Going Forward

14. Think of one or two things you have learned that you'd like to work on in the coming week. Remember that this is all about quality, not quantity. It's better to work on one specific area of life and do it well than to work on many and do poorly (or to be so overwhelmed that you simply don't try).

Do you need to develop your prayer life? Do you need to learn how to better salt your speech with grace? Be specific. Go back through Colossians 4:2–18 and put a star next to the phrase or verse that is most encouraging to you. Consider memorizing this verse.

Real-Life Application Ideas: Write letters to people who had an early and positive impact on your faith life, thanking them for their willingness to reach out and support you. Then spend a little time in prayer for each of these people before you deliver the letters.

Seeking Help

15. Write a prayer below (or simply pray one in silence), inviting God to work on your mind and heart in those areas you've previously noted. Be honest about your desires and fears.

Notes for Small Groups:

- *Look for ways to put into practice the things you wrote in the Going Forward section in this lesson. Talk with other group members about your ideas and commit to being accountable to one another.*

- *During the coming week, ask the Holy Spirit to continue to reveal truth to you from what you've read and studied.*

Summary and Review

Notes for Small Groups: This session is a summary and review of this study. Because of that, it is shorter than the previous lessons. If you are using this in a small-group setting, consider combining this lesson with a time of fellowship or a shared meal.

Before you begin…
- *Pray for the Holy Spirit to reveal truth and wisdom as you go through this lesson.*
- *Briefly review the notes you made in the previous sessions. You will refer back to previous sections throughout this bonus lesson.*

Looking Back

1. Over the past eight lessons, you've examined Paul's letter to the Colossians. What expectations did you bring to this study? In what ways were these expectations met?

2. What is the most significant personal discovery you've made from this study?

3. What surprised you most about Paul's focus on the preeminence of Christ? Why do you think he spent so much of the letter on this theme? How does this letter help Christians better understand Christ's role in their lives?

Progress Report

4. Take a few moments to review the Going Forward sections of the previous lessons. How would you rate your progress for each of the things you chose to work on? What adjustments, if any, do you need to make to continue on the path toward spiritual maturity?

5. In what ways have you grown closer to Christ during this study? Take a moment to celebrate these things. Then think of areas where you feel you still need to grow and note those here. Make plans to revisit this study in a few weeks to review your growing faith.

Things to Pray About

6. Colossians is theological letter as well as one full of encouragement. As you reflect on the words Paul has written, ask God to reveal to you those truths that you most need to hear. Revisit the book often, and seek the Holy Spirit's guidance to gain a better understanding of what it means to be in relationship with Jesus.

7. Colossians explores important themes, including a contrast between the "new life" and the "old ways," the centrality of Christ, and lots of practical

relational advice—particularly regarding families. Spend time praying about each of these topics.

8. Whether you've been studying this in a small group or on your own, there are many other Christians working through the very same issues you discovered when examining Paul's letter to the Colossians. Take time to pray for each of them, that God would reveal truth, that the Holy Spirit would guide them, and that each person might grow in spiritual maturity according to God's will.

A Blessing of Encouragement

Studying the Bible is one of the best ways to learn how to be more like Christ. Thanks for taking this step. In closing, let this blessing precede you and follow you into the next week while you continue to marinate in God's Word:

May God light your path to greater understanding as you review the truths found in the book of Colossians and consider how they can help you grow closer to Christ.